Drayton Island:
An Illustrated History

by

Walt Grampp and Kevin McCarthy

2016

ISBN-13: 978-1532918896

ISBN-10: 1532918895

Printed in the United States of America

Acknowledgments

Among the people we wish to thank in the writing of this book are residents Ronnie and Bruce Geiger, Kay and Herman "Buddy" Honecker, Deanne Clark and Bill Jeter Jr. Also Karelisa Hartigan for her careful copy-editing, the librarians at the Putnam County Public Library in Palatka, and the archivists at the University of Florida Library.

The illustration on the cover is an aerial view of Drayton Island from LABINS: Land Boundary Information System. Used with permission.

CONTENTS

Photos of Drayton Island today

A long dock extending to the St. Johns River

A boathouse at the end of one of the island docks

INTRODUCTION

Boaters heading south on the St. Johns River from the small town of Welaka or north from Lake George will come upon Drayton Island, the largest island in the river. The privately owned, heavily wooded island, which is about 1700 acres in size, lies just west of the channel of the river, which is one of the relatively few rivers in the world which runs north.

In a way, the history of the island resembles that of the Florida peninsula as a whole. That history includes early settlement by Native Americans; attempts at colonization by the British and maybe the French and Spanish; the growing of citrus by intrepid farmers; the building of houses by full-time and part-time residents; even speculation by investors who had plans of development with the help of an airstrip.

Co-authors Walt Grampp (left)
& Kevin McCarthy
on Drayton Island in 2016

The co-authors have spent much time on the river and on Drayton Island. Walter Grampp's parents first came to the island in the early 20th century and built a house there. Walt still lives there part of the year. Kevin McCarthy boated the whole St. Johns in 2007, from the swamps and beginning of the waterway near Vero Beach to its mouth at Mayport.

We're hoping that several different types of readers will find this work of use: those who live on the island or have relatives there or who have lived or visited there in the past; those who enjoy reading about out-of-the way, fascinating places in our remarkable state; those who work in genealogy (we have included the 1880 census of the island); and those who like regional history. If readers find any mistakes, please contact the authors by email;
Kevin McCarthy: ceyhankevin@gmail.com
Walt Grampp: waltgrampp@gmail.com

If there is enough interest for a second edition, we will make any necessary corrections.

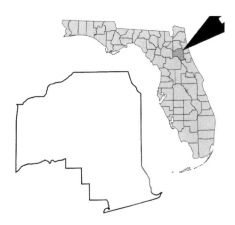

A map of Putnam County, Florida, where Drayton Island is located. The black arrow points to the county, which is in the northeastern part of the state. The image to the left of the outline of Florida is the outline of Putnam County.

Chapter One: The Location and Size of the Island

Drayton Island is about twenty miles south of Palatka, nine miles southwest of Crescent City, thirty-one miles north of De-Land, and thirty-two miles east of Ocala, Florida. The island is just north of Lake George and about 105 miles from the mouth of the St. Johns River at Mayport.

The most important feature of Drayton Island is the St. Johns River, which surrounds the island on four sides. The St. Johns is the most important river in Florida, whether from a historical or commercial or recreational point of view. Its 310 miles have seen some of the most important people in our state's history: Jean Ribault, John and William Bartram, Zephaniah Kingsley Jr., John James Audubon, Winslow Homer, Frederick Delius, Harriet Beecher Stowe, and Marjorie Kinnan Rawlings, as well as many important groups: Native Americans like the Timucua and Seminoles, runaway slaves, British and Spanish settlers, missionaries, and thousands of migrating settlers who came here for a better life.

The St. Johns River, indicated by the black squiggly line on the right of this image, is the major river in the history of Florida.

The history of the river is similar to that of Florida in terms of the people who lived along the river and used its many resources, including the native peoples who lived in many settlements along the river and used it for transportation and fishing; the French, British, and Spanish who fought on the river for domination of the whole peninsula; and the many Americans who have lived along the river and used it for generations.

Others include the early tourists who boated the river to find relief from northern winters; the settlers who entered the region to find a new beginning to raise their families and earn a living; and the modern residents who came for the river's commerce and recreation.

Drayton Island lies just north of Lake George, the second-largest lake in Florida – after Lake Okeechobee. Lake George, which John Bartram, the royal British botanist, named around 1765 after King George III of England, is about eleven miles long and six miles wide with an average depth of eight feet. The name of the lake dates back to the two decades (1763 – 1783) when the British occupied East Florida.

John Bartram, the royal botanist for Great Britain

Boaters using Lake George need to be especially careful and on the lookout for the fierce storms that can arise very quickly on the huge body of water. The lake is very popular in the summer as boaters use it to visit several springs on the western shore which lead into the lake: Juniper Creek, Silver Glen, and Salt. (See map on next page.)

The uninhabited Hog Island lies off the northwestern part of Drayton Island. From time to time, speculators make ambitious plans to develop Hog Island with houses and recreational facilities, but nothing has yet come of those plans.

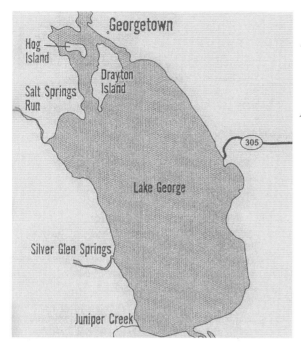

Drayton Island and the much smaller Hog Island lie just north of the large Lake George, out of which the St. Johns River continues flowing north.

The name of Hog Island may date back to a time when hogs roamed the site, but they are apparently no longer there. (More about Hog Island on p. 16.)

The St. Johns River splits around Drayton Island. The waters to the west of the island are not deep, but shallow-draft boats can maneuver there. Drayton Island is about 2.5 miles long and one mile wide. The topography varies from low wetland areas at sea level to upland areas with an elevation of twelve to fifteen feet.

As can be seen in newspaper comments from the nineteenth and twentieth centuries, the beauty and charm of the island have long attracted visitors and residents alike.

A long, dirt road runs from the ferry landing at the northern part of the island south, south-west to the southern part. In the past, Putnam County officials have asked the homeowners if they want that dirt road paved, but the majority have said no.

That road may have been part of an airplane runway that used to allow visitors/owners to land their planes on the island instead of relying on boat transportation. Relatively few planes landed on the runway, but it was there for those who had the means to fly onto the island.

The dirt road used to be a runway on the island.

The 20-foot-wide county road parallels the eastern shore and lies 600 to 2800 feet from the shore. It is the only public roadway on the island. Many unpaved streets, which run to the residences on the island, connect with this main road. The main road and the unpaved streets that run to the houses are sometimes flooded in heavy rains.

About a dozen or so people live on the island all year round, while another twenty+ live there part time, especially during the pleasant spring and fall months. The island has approximately two dozen single-family houses, which are connected to the one dirt road by long driveways. Many of the houses cannot be seen from the dirt road. Most houses are on the river on the east side of the island, and some of those houses have docks that extend out into the river.

One can see pilings of former docks that may have allowed large, passing boats to tie up and load/unload goods and passengers. Severe storms from the east or south off Lake George have destroyed those docks and any boathouses on the end of the docks. (More about the role of steamships and the island in Chapter Six.)

A long, wide dock from the island out into the St. Johns River

The island was well suited for the growing of crops. *The Palatka Daily News* of the 1880s had regular reports of farmers on the island growing cabbages, cucumbers, oranges, potatoes, and squash. Old photographs show food stuffs being kept at the end of docks for pick-up by passing steamboats.

While most of the island consists of land suitable for growing crops, a large wetland area of about 140 acres lies in the center of the island. That marshy area does not seem capable of sustaining the growing of crops or the building of houses.

The agricultural use of the island, in fact, was an important reason why so many people over the decades have been interested in owning the island, going back to Zephaniah Kingsley Jr. in the early nineteenth century. However, freezes did occasionally occur on the island, as we will see in Chapter Six.

The ferry landing on Drayton Island

The ferry landing at the northern part of the island is about five feet above sea level, having been formed with fill dirt put there for the building of the ferry dock. Near that dock is a collection of mail boxes, allowing the mail carrier to deposit the mail for all the residents.

Most homeowners seem to have wells for water, as well as septic tanks. Some have cisterns to collect rainwater that drains into large holding tanks. A few homeowners have water-retention ponds that collect water before machines clean it and pump it to the houses. Salt intrusion in the wells has been a problem. Marine cables take electricity from Georgetown on the mainland through cables under the channel and onto the island, where poles take the electricity to individual homes.

A retention pond on the island for collecting water

Once a week, garbage trucks from the mainland cross over on the ferry and pick up the garbage along the main road. Weeds, hydrilla, and cattails are a constant problem, and some residents make a concerted effort to keep the water near their docks clear of the growth.

From time to time, entrepreneurs have proposed the development of the island, for example the building of a marina to take advantage of the proximity of the river and Lake George, but nothing has come of that.

Because the island has no stores or beaches or touristic attractions, casual visitors are discouraged from visiting the site. In fact, the ferry driver will often ask strangers: "Which residents are you planning to visit?" If the visitor is vague or not planning on visiting anyone in particular, the operator of the ferry will politely try to discourage such casual visitors. He might also say: "I can get you onto the island, but I don't guarantee that I can get you off."

The closest town to Drayton Island is Georgetown on the mainland to the east. That is where one can take the ferry across to Drayton Island. The population of Georgetown in 2014 was 1,077 people. More about the development of the town in subsequent chapters.

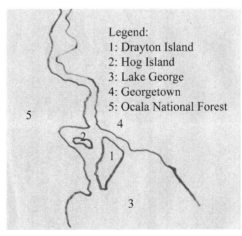

Legend:
1: Drayton Island
2: Hog Island
3: Lake George
4: Georgetown
5: Ocala National Forest

A map of the area showing the two islands,
Lake George, Georgetown, and the Ocala National Forest

Another major geographical factor in the history and development of Drayton Island is the Ocala National Forest to the west of the island. The huge plot of land, established as a national forest in 1908 by President Theodore Roosevelt, is the oldest national forest east of the Mississippi River and the southernmost national forest in the continental United States. It covers 607 square miles of central Florida and has a vast array of wildlife and fauna.

The Ocala National Forest lies between the St. Johns River and the Ocklawaha River, hosts many visitors each year, and offers a wide range of activities, including birdwatching, camping, fishing, hiking, or boating.

Visitors can cross the St. Johns River to the Ocala National Forest on the Fort Gates Ferry, which is headquartered between Lake George and Little Lake George at Fruitland Cove.

The Fort Gates Ferry, pictured here in 2016,
crosses the St. Johns River.

Animals on the island

Wild animals live on the island, including an occasional bear that must have swum over from the mainland in search of food. Some hunters and homeowners have shot annoying raccoons, squirrels, and deer that tipped over garbage cans and ate the garden-produced vegetables, but most residents are content to let the animals have their own space.

Residents over the years have seen an occasional rattlesnake, and at least one resident claimed to have a python, but a little care and shuffling while walking will scare the snakes away. Local residents report that famed herpetologist Ross Allen (1908 – 1981) came to Drayton Island to collect rattlesnakes; Allen established the Reptile Institute in Silver Springs, Florida, to study alligators, crocodiles, and snakes. Some residents reported that snakes, which were much more common in the past, would actually fall out of trees as people walked along – a scary experience.

Many birds nest on the island or use it as part of their migration patterns.

12

Photos of other animals on the island

Raccoon

Armadillo

A river cooter

A Florida Softshell Turtle

One particularly annoying critter is the so-called "blind mosquito," an aquatic midge that resembles a mosquito in appearance, but which does not bite or suck blood or carry diseases. Larvae live on Lake George itself, so it would be impossible to poison them, even if one wanted to do so. Man-made ponds or standing water can lead to infestations of the pests, and most people agree that, if the flies did bite or suck one's blood, living on the island would be very difficult. The island also has its share of ticks.

The St Joseph Herald (Saint Joseph, Michigan) in January, 1886, reported that the island had red bats.

An eastern red bat

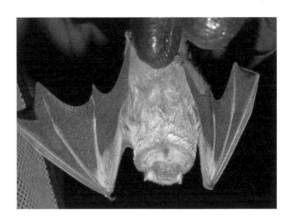

The channel that allows bigger vessels to travel on the St. Johns lies to the east of Drayton Island and is clearly marked with lighted buoys at night, although very few vessels use the river at night. The channel is about ten feet deep. Those crossing the channel to go to and from the island have to take care that no other boat, especially a speed boat, is traveling in the area. The river, of course, runs north to Jacksonville and connects with the Atlantic Ocean at Mayport, Florida, after about 105 miles.

Hog Island

The island off the northwest shore of Drayton Island, Hog Island, may have been named for wild hogs that once roamed there. Hog Island is mentioned in *Our Place in Time: A Chronology of Putnam County*, when José Coppinger, governor of East Florida from 1816 to 1821, gave one Francis Richard in 1818 a grant of 1,025 acres on the west side of Lake George, including an island "in a cove on the west side of Lake George opposite the western coast of 'Dryton or Kingley [sic] Island (Florence McLean's Isla, or Hog Island) north of the mouth of the Big Salt Spring...."

Later in the same book Hog Island is described as follows: "300 acres at the entrance of Lake George, is too low to cultivate but has fine timber growth. Drayton Island is 4 to 15 feet above sea level." (p. 94)

In the last decade or so, some would-be developers have examined Hog Island and made ambitious plans to develop what they called "a forgotten paradise" with the help of famous angler Gadabout Gaddis, the star of the television show "Flying Fisherman." The brochure that the developers produced (see image to the left) had ambitious plans of building skillfully crafted cabins on the island, but nothing has come of it, possibly because the island is too low in elevation.

Chapter Two: The First Inhabitants in the Area

Around 50,000 years ago, much of the earth's waters was frozen in glaciers, and the level of the oceans was as much as 350 feet lower than today. The North American continent was joined to Asia at the Bering Strait west of where Alaska is today.

Asian hunters made their way across the land bridge, which scientists call Beringia, to look for animals like the giant mastodon and mammoth. The hunters spread out over all of North America and settled down with their families in places where they could hunt and fish.

Large mammoths like these used to roam through Florida, as evidenced by their bones and fossils found in phosphate pits and deep springs, for example Wakulla Springs near Tallahassee.

About 12,000 years ago, some of those people reached Florida. Archaeologists call those first Floridians Paleoindians. Those Native Americans chose to live in places where they could hunt, fish, raise crops, and support their families.

The St. Johns River offered many suitable places for the Native Americans to flourish. The area had forests full of plants and animals; rivers and lakes that had fish and turtles; proximity to the ocean with its vast numbers of fish, turtles, and shellfish; and the ability to travel to offshore islands in large canoes.

When Juan Ponce de León and his followers arrived on the Atlantic coast of northeast Florida in 1513 at Pascua Florida, the Easter season, the Florida peninsula had at least 250,000 Indians, who were grouped into some one hundred different tribes.

According to archaeologists like Jerald Milanich, one of the major Indian tribes in north Florida in the sixteenth and seventeenth centuries, for example along the St. Johns, was the Timucua. Other groups were the Apalachee in the northwestern part of the peninsula and the Calusa in the southwest.

Above is an engraving by Theodorus de Bry (1528 – 1598),
who never came to America, but who primarily based his
images on the descriptions of an artist, Jacques Le Moyne, who did
come here with René Laudonnière in 1564; this picture shows Native
Americans in disguise near a body of water in Florida as they stalk
deer. The body of water may resemble the St. Johns River.

One of the subgroups of the Timucua were the Utina/Outina. Below is an engraving by De Bry, done in 1591, which shows an Outina chief consulting with a so-called sorcerer before going to battle. The notes for the engraving are these: "The sorcerer kneels on a shield surrounded with signs scratched in the ground. He contorts himself in an effort to determine the strength of the enemy."

A major clue to the presence of Native Americans in Florida is the shell mound, also known as a tumulus, platform mound, burial mound, and midden. While there used to be thousands of such mounds in Florida, road-builders have leveled many of them and used the compacted shell remnants for the roads. Or developers have leveled the mounds, before such practice was forbidden by law, to build in their places luxurious houses. A major midden which has survived along the St. Johns River is at Mount Royal, which is several miles north of Drayton Island on the east shore of the river.

We know about the presence of Native Americans like the Timucua at Mount Royal and also at Drayton Island from the observations of John Bartram (1699 – 1777), the King's Botanist for North America in the employ of British King George III.

John's son, William (1739 – 1823), was even more famous as a collector of plant specimens and as one who traveled through the Southeast, including Florida.

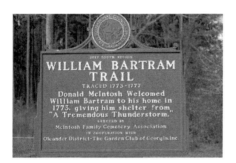

Trail markers for the William Bartram Trail, like this one to the left, are located throughout the Southeast.

As John Bartram wrote in his *Diary of a Journey through the Carolinas, Georgia, and Florida*, he and his party arrived at Mount Royal on January 25, 1766, and found a large "Indian tumulus, which was about 100 yards in diameter, nearly round, and near twenty feet high; found some bones scattered on it. It must be ancient, as there are live oaks growing upon it three foot in diameter."

Archaeologist Clarence B. Moore excavated at Mount Royal in 1893 and 1894 and found in addition to the burial mound used by Native Americans a village area, earthworks, and the remnants of a Spanish mission called San Antonio de Anacape, which served the local Timucua Indians.

Moore and his team found a copper breast-plate, polished stone tools, pearl and shell beads, and decorated ceramic vessels. They estimated that Native Americans built the mound between A.D. 1250 and 1500. Jesuit missionaries built the mission before leaving in 1572. Franciscan missionaries used the site from 1573 to 1587.

Archaeologist B. Calvin Jones also excavated at the village site in 1983 and in 1994-1995, finding more buildings that contained Spanish artifacts and were part of the Mission of San Antonio de Anacape (1587–1675).

The historic plaque at the site is near the large midden.

Archaeologist Jerald Milanich noted in his book entitled *Famous Florida Sites: Mount Royal and Crystal River* that famed archaeologist Clarence B. Moore (1852 – 1936) explored 83 Indian mounds along the St. Johns River.

One can guess at the extensive size of the Mount Royal mound by looking at what is left, although visitors should not walk on the mound.

Among those mounds, he did extensive work at Mount Royal. That site was placed on the National Register of Historic Places and is officially owned by the State of Florida. Today it is about 1.1 acres in size. The causeway and middens are privately owned, but a kiosk on the site has a good explanation of the important Indian site, which today is several hundred yards from the St. Johns River.

Archaeologists estimate that Native Americans occupied the Mount Royal site beginning in the Late Archaic period (3,000 – 500 B.C.). Scientists call it a mound center, meaning that it was the center of a number of Indian groups.

A kiosk at the site of Mount Royal explains its significance for the Native Americans of the area.

The tall mound that one can still see at the site may have indicated the importance of the local chief and his ancestors and descendants. The mound, which the Native Americans there considered a holy place, contained the mortal remains of the important members of the tribe.

The high point of the importance of Mount Royal was between A.D. 1050 and 1300, well before the arrival of the Europeans.

While Mount Royal was probably the main site of Native Americans in that area along the St. Johns River, archaeologists have also found at least two Indian mounds on Drayton Island.

Keith Ashley in *The Florida Anthropologist* and others argue that the sixteenth-century Timucua village of Edelano was on Drayton Island and that one could actually see a large circle in aerial views at one point, a circle that was 364 meters in diameter, but that may have been destroyed in subsequent development in the early twentieth century. Some think that a vegetative growth pattern is also discernible. One scholar in the same article believes that two parallel ridges about 15 – 20 centimeters high are the remains of the causeway that the Bartrams saw.

For more about the visit to Drayton Island by John Bartram's son, William, see Chapter Five.

Timucua Indians having a conference

In *The Florida Anthropologist* Keith Ashley argued that both "archaeological and documentary evidence" link "the Mt. Royal site and the early seventeenth-century mission-period village of San Antonio de Anacape." (p. 279) He argues that the Mount Royal Native-American site was abandoned around A.D. 1300 and that the seat of local power shifted – with the people moving south to Drayton Island.

It is possible that the long avenue described by the Bartrams joined the Indian mounds in the north of the island with a distant pond that acted as a "borrow pit," from which the dirt for the mound fill was taken.

Could it have been possible that the low-lying, swampy area of Drayton Island in the middle of the island (see map below – with black arrows pointing out the swamp/marsh) was the site of the borrow pit?

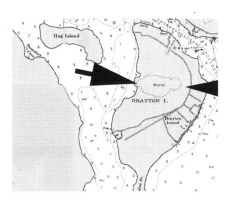

That the dirt for the mounds was originally excavated by the Native Americans from that site? It may be too late for archaeological digging at the swamp to determine the answers to these questions, but the possibilities are intriguing.

Within two hundred years of the arrival of the Spaniards in Florida in 1513, the weapons and diseases of the Europeans had killed millions of Native Americans in the New World, including the Florida peninsula.

Many Indians also died after the Spaniards took them away from their tribes to carry the supplies that the Spanish army was taking with it. Also, because the Spanish soldiers stole food from the Indians along the way, many Native American tribes faced severe food shortages after the Spanish passed through their territory.

This image by Theodorus De Bry shows Florida Native Americans treating the sick among them.

The picture above by De Bry shows a Florida Indian family crossing a river, perhaps the St. Johns, on their way to an island, perhaps Drayton. The woman carries the children and the food, while the male Indian carries his bow and arrows for protection. He has his quiver on top of his head in order to keep his arrows dry.

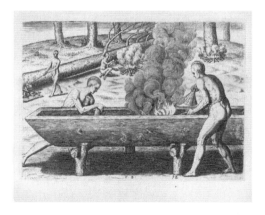

Here De Bry shows Native Americans making a canoe by burning a log and using scrapers to hollow it out.

*Theodorus de Bry here illustrates a small party
of Native Americans rowing a canoe with articles in the boat.*

*This engraving by Theodorus de Bry shows how the Timucua
killed a sentinel for falling asleep while on duty.*

Chapter Three: Sixteenth Century

The French in Florida

In 1513, Juan Ponce de León and his Spanish followers landed in northeast Florida, claimed "La Florida" for Spain, and sailed away without establishing any colony there. About five decades later, in 1562, French Huguenot colonists left France looking for a place to practice their religion without fear of persecution and arrived in what is today northeast Florida.

Their leader, Jean Ribault (1520 – 1565), with the assistance of René Goulaine de Laudonnière (c. 1529 – 1574), claimed the territory for France, but eventually went north to found Charlesfort on Parris Island, South Carolina. While in Florida, Ribault had erected a stone monument on the St. Johns Bluff over the river. The difficulties of establishing a viable settlement in South Carolina induced the French to abandon their efforts and return to France.

A replica of the Ribault Monument near the St. Johns River

Two years later, in 1564, Laudonnière led a group of French colonists back to Florida, where they established Fort Caroline in what they called the Rivière de Mai, or River of May, so called because Ribault had arrived there on the first of May. They built a fortification, Fort Caroline, in the river, now called the St. Johns. The fort, which has long been lost, has been reconstructed on the nearby land.

The reconstructed Fort Caroline

Stefan Lorant in *The New World* has a narrative description of an expedition the French sent up the St. Johns River, which they called "Rivière de Mai," up to Lake George and then back past what they called Edelano, which is present-day Drayton Island: "I sent the two shallops on an exploring expedition up the river, which they ascended for thirty miles above Mathiaca [present-day site unknown]. They discovered a lake [probably modern-day Lake George] so wide that its farther shore could not be seen from the top of the tallest tree on this side. For this reason they did not attempt to go any farther, but returned by way of Chilili [present-day site unknown].

Here, in the middle of the river, they found Edelano, the most delightful island in the world. It is a populous island about three miles square, abounding in fruits. Between the town of Edelano and the riverside there is a walk three hundred yards long and fifteen wide bordered by great trees whose over-arching branches form a vaulting that seems to be constructed, not by nature, but by art, and has, perhaps, no equal in the world."

When the Spanish returned to the New World and found that the French had established Fort Caroline, the former marched overland from St. Augustine, destroyed Fort Caroline, killed any Frenchmen they could find, then sailed south to the Matanzas Inlet south of St. Augustine, and slaughtered most of the Frenchmen they found there.

The Frenchmen had sailed out into the ocean from Fort Caroline, but a severe storm blew them south and shipwrecked them – before the Spanish found them and killed them at Matanzas. The word "Matanzas" means "slaughters" in Spanish.

Matanzas Inlet today is quite serene – without any trace of the slaughter that took place there.

As John McGrath points out in his book, *The French in Early Florida,* the hurricane that blew the French ships south and away from St. Augustine led to "a decisive, crushing defeat that effectively ended any French challenges to Spanish America for decades." (p. 169)

McGrath speculates that, if the French had defeated the Spanish in Florida instead of the other way around, the Spanish might have been forced to settle lands north of Florida. That might have prevented the English from colonizing Virginia and New England.

The New World would have looked very different, and the subsequent history of the American colonies would have differed drastically from what it was. And all because of a hurricane that hit St. Augustine in 1565.

The successful attack by Pedro Menéndez de Avilés and his Spanish forces effectively ended the French attempts to colonize Florida.

Chapter Four: Seventeenth Century

The Spanish and the Native Americans in Florida

Many Spanish missionaries established missions in Florida to subdue and convert the Native Americans they met there. In doing so, the Catholic missionaries tried to force the Indians to give up their native customs, beliefs, and lifestyles in favor of European mores, but the efforts of the Europeans had only limited success. While Drayton Island was further south than most of the Catholic missions established in La Florida, missionaries may have gone up the St. Johns River to reach distant tribes.

A reconstructed council house at the Mission San Luis near Tallahassee

There is no indication or artifact found indicating that the Spanish established such a mission on or near Drayton Island, but it is possible. Michael Gannon in *The Cross in the Sand* (p. 148) wrote that a Catholic missionary "made several mission trips to the commercial and plantation villages that were sprouting along the St. Johns River and the Atlantic shore," including Palatka, but whether the missionaries made it down as far as Drayton Island is unclear.

John Worth in *The Timucua Chiefdoms of Spanish Florida* wrote about the bad situation of the Native Americans in Florida: "By the last quarter of the seventeenth century … aboriginal populations in this same region either had been reduced to a chain of small mission towns along the primary road through the Spanish colonial administrative district known as the Timucua province, or they had aggregated as fugitives in several remote areas beyond effective Spanish control." (Preface)

In the last part of the seventeenth century, the Spaniards had a new worry: the influx of British forces in settlements north of St. Augustine. The British had established outposts in North and South Carolina and then began moving southward into Spanish Florida, where they came into conflict with the Spaniards and their Indian allies.

Theodorus De Bry made an engraving that showed
the Timucua roasting animals, maybe small gators.

The Native Americans from the Carolinas attacked the Florida Indians in order to capture the latter and make them slaves. The Carolina Indians had guns, something that the Florida Indians did not have, and so the battles were often very unequal. The seventeenth century was a hard one for Florida Native Americans, and thousands of them died from diseases and battles.

Chapter Five: Eighteenth Century

In the early eighteenth century, the British, who had established settlements along the eastern coast of North America, continued their attacks on Spanish settlements in Florida. Because La Florida was so far away from Spain, the Spanish in Florida had a difficult time protecting their settlements and supplying them with food and ammunition.

By the middle of the eighteenth century, relatively few Native Americans were left in Florida. Thousands had been killed by diseases and battles with Europeans and with other Native Americans. Only several thousand remained from the hundreds of thousands who had lived here for thousands of years.

A Seminole spearing a garfish from a dugout in Florida, 1930

One group of runaways who joined the relatively few remaining Seminoles in Florida were black slaves escaping from the brutal life on plantations north of Florida. The Seminoles usually welcomed the runaway slaves because they realized that the blacks knew the languages of the white people and therefore could help translate for the Indians. The blacks also knew how to use the latest farming methods, which they had learned on the plantations. Sometimes the blacks married Seminoles and produced what researchers have called Black Seminoles.

One such Black Seminole was called "Negro Abraham," a leader of the Black Seminoles.

Negro Abraham

The Spanish controlled Florida for all of the seventeenth and eighteenth centuries except for two decades (1763 – 1783), when the British controlled it. At the end of the eighteenth century, the Spanish were back in control of "La Florida," and the Seminoles were doing well. The nineteenth century, however, would negatively affect both the Spanish and Seminoles living in Florida.

The Seminoles may have been living on Drayton Island during those centuries, but archaeologists have not yet found definitive proof in the form of artifacts.

William Drayton, the namesake of Drayton Island

In an article about William Drayton, author Charles Mowat called Drayton, the chief justice of British East Florida, an erudite and stubborn jurist who was born in America and had strong sympathies for the Americans in their fight for independence from England. He found himself in a British province (East Florida) that did not allow its citizens representation in the British Parliament.

He was born in 1732 at Magnolia, a plantation in South Carolina. After receiving his legal training in London, England, he returned to South Carolina and served for six years in the assembly there. In 1765, when the first chief justice of East Florida, James Moultrie, died, Florida Governor James Grant appointed Drayton temporarily to the position and recommended him for the permanent position.

Drayton did not achieve the permanent position immediately, but within three years (1768) became chief justice and moved his family to St. Augustine. While he was chief justice, he began acquiring much land in East Florida, including Drayton Island. In May 1771, Governor Grant was succeeded by John Moultrie, who would serve as governor until March 1774. Moultrie and Drayton clashed on many issues.

James Grant served as Governor of East Florida from 1763 to 1771.

Governor Moultrie was succeeded by Governor Patrick Tonyn, who served from 1774 until 1784 and who was also the brunt of many criticisms by Chief Justice Drayton. For example, Drayton accused the governor of untruthfulness, waste of public funds, unpunctuality in making payments, and creating a monopoly in beef for a favored profiteer.

The governor in turn accused Drayton of being sympathetic to the Americans' cause for independence and had him suspended from office. Although reinstated in office, Drayton eventually despaired of being able to work with the British government, resigned his position, and went to South Carolina, where he was made a judge of the Admiralty Court of the State of South Carolina, an associate justice of the Supreme Court of South Carolina, and the first judge of the U.S. District Court for South Carolina.

He died in debt in 1790, partly because he had not received any compensation for the lands he had bought in East Florida, which must have included Drayton Island.

Today's Magnolia Plantation, which William Drayton's family built in South Carolina and where he died in 1790

Drayton Island in 1766 and 1774

Two very important visitors to the island during the two decades (1763 – 1783) that the British controlled Florida were John Bartram (1699 – 1777) and his son William (1739 – 1823). John, the Royal Botanist for King George III of England, took William on a five hundred-mile trip through East Florida that lasted for several months in the winter of 1765 – 1766.

Throughout that journey of the Bartrams, John examined the plants, trees, and soil and kept a journal, while William sketched pictures of the plants and animals, especially the birds.

*A sketch of John Bartram
by Howard Pyle*

Members of the Bartram Society have carefully looked at the journals that the Bartrams kept and surmised the route that they took. When the Bartrams came to Drayton Island, they seem to have stayed on the west side of the island northwest of Lake George.

Several years ago the Bartram Society erected plaques at those places which the members determined were associated with the Bartrams.

For more information about the Bartram Trail see this web site: http://bartram.putnam-fl.com/.

While we cannot be absolutely sure about the exact location of the campsites that the Bartrams used on Drayton Island, members of the Bartram Society have carefully looked at the topography of the island and matched that with the entries in the journals that the Bartrams kept. Those members have determined that the place where the Bartrams stayed on the west side of the island may now be under water – with the constant erosion that the island has undergone.

Consequently, the Bartram Society has erected a post about a hundred yards offshore. On that post one can see the notation "Putnam County Bartram Trail. B[artram] T[rail] 24. Drayton Island 1766 Camp. Private Property." A bar code on the sign should allow those with a Smart Phone app to hear more about the site. Again, it is private property, and therefore visitors should not go onto the land there. The Society received permission from the landowner to put up the plaque, pictured below.

The wooden post marking the spot of the Bartrams'
1766 camp at Drayton Island

William, John's son, journeyed up the St. Johns River in 1774 on his extensive travels in Florida. He also visited Drayton Island and referred to the Native Americans in the area. William wrote: "The island seems to be the residence of an Indian Prince." Bartram also thought he noticed the traces of a large town that the Native Americans had used, but he saw no inhabitants at that time.

The cover of the book that William Bartram wrote about his travels in the Southeast, including Florida

Bartram wrote the following about Drayton Island, which was called Bryan's Island, perhaps after an early owner of the island. Bartram described the island as being "about two miles in breadth, and three quarters of a mile where broadest, mostly high land, well timbered, and fertile." (p. 103 of Mark Van Doren's edition)

He then went on to describe Drayton Island, which he called a "princely island": "The island appears, from obvious vestiges, to have been once the chosen residence of an Indian prince, there being to this day evident remains of a large town of the Aborigines."

"It was situated on an eminence near the banks of the lake, and commanded a comprehensive and charming prospect of the waters, islands, east and west shores of the lake [Lake George], the capes, the bay, and Mount Royal; and to the south, the view is in a manner infinite, where the skies and waters seem to unite.

On the site of this ancient town, stands an impressive Indian mound, or conical pyramid of earth, from which runs in a straight line a grand avenue or Indian highway, through a magnificent grove of magnolias, live oaks, palms, and orange trees, terminating at the verge of a large green level savanna."

One of several high Indian mounds at the northern part of the island may have been the site of the Indian village. The mounds, which are full of thousands of small shells, have been falling into the river as the shoreline recedes.

[Continuation of Bartram's description:] "This island appears to have been well inhabited, as is very evident, from the quantities of fragments of Indian earthen ware, bones of animals and other remains, particularly in the shelly heights and ridges all over the island.

Native-American artifacts like these have been found on the island, especially in the northern part near the Indian mounds.

There are no habitations at present on the island, but a great number of deer, turkeys, bears, wolves, wild cats, squirrels, racoons [sic], and opossums. The bears are invited here to partake of the fruit of the orange tree, which they are immoderately fond of; and both they and turkeys are made extremely fat and delicious, from their feeding on the sweet acorns of the live oak."

[Continuation of Bartram's description after a paragraph describing some of the flowers there:] "There are some rich swamps on the shores of the island, and these are verged on the outside with large marshes, covered entirely with tall grass, rushes, and herbaceous plants; amongst these are several species of Hibiscus, particularly the hibiscus coccineus. This most stately of all herbaceous plants grows ten or twelve feet high, branching regularly, so as to form a sharp cone. These branches also divide again, and are embellished with large expanded crimson flowers.

The island still has a dense, rich foliage.

I have seen this plant of the size and figure of a beautiful little tree, having at once several hundred of these splendid flowers, which may be then seen at a great distance. They continue to flower in succession all summer and autumn, when the stems wither and decay; but the perennial root sends forth new stems the next spring, and so on for many years...." (pp. 104 – 105)

[Continuation of Bartram's description of the island:] "Having finished my tour on this princely island, I prepared for repose. A calm evening had succeeded the stormy day.

The late tumultuous winds had now ceased, the face of the lake had become placid, and the skies serene; the balmy winds breathed the animating odours of the groves around me; and as I reclined on the elevated banks of the lake, at the foot of a live oak, I enjoyed the prospect of its wide waters, its fringed coasts, and the distant horizon.

The squadrons of aquatic fowls, emerging out of the water, and hastening to their leafy coverts on shore, closed the varied scenes of the past day. I was lulled asleep by the mixed sounds of the wearied surf, laping [sic] on the hard beaten shore, and the tender warblings of the painted nonpareil and other winged inhabitants of the grove." (p. 106)

An eagle's nest on the island in the recent past

As with the 1766 camp site of the Bartrams, we cannot be absolutely sure where William Bartram camped on the island on his 1774 trip. Based on a careful reading of William's journal, members of the local Bartram Society went to the waters off the eastern shore of the island, waded into the water from an offshore boat, and nailed to a tree a plaque designating the place where they thought William must have stayed.

A plaque designates the 1774 camp site of William Bartram.

The words are similar to the plaque on the west side, except that the east side one has: "Drayton Island 1774 Camp."

Again, the area is privately owned, and therefore visitors should not trespass. Boaters need to be aware that the depth of the water near the 1774 plaque is very shallow. We owe a debt of gratitude to the members of the Bartram Society for the care they have taken to identify such places associated with John and William Bartram.

Chapter Six: Nineteenth Century

The Spanish and Americans in Florida

In 1804, Governor Enrique White, who was governor of East Florida from June 1796 until March 1811, granted a plot of 1500 acres on Drayton Island to George Sibbald for the raising of coffee. Authorities allowed Sibbald to use ten African-Americans at the start of the coffee-growing, but – as the trees grew – he could use more such workers. However, if the local Seminole Indians objected, the contract would be invalid. The Spanish stopped giving land grants, like the one to Sibbald, in 1818.

When George Sibbald died, for some reason his estate owed Zephaniah Kingsley Jr. $3,381 for renting out African-Americans from 1805 through 1811 to improve Drayton Island, four sacks of seed coffee, the pay of the overseers (Mr. Manton and Samuel Toms), and provisions. Sibbald's widow (?), Jane, agreed to the bill, but could not pay it directly. Instead, she had to pay it in installments. Kingsley could agree to receive profits from the sale of Drayton Island products or could take over the whole island as full payment. On July 18, 1811, Kingsley took over control of the island.

A map of Florida showing Drayton Island (#1) and Kingsley Plantation (#2 north of Drayton Island)

In 1821, the United States took control of Florida from the Spanish. On July 7, 1821, Governor José Coppinger gave title to the island to Zephaniah Kingsley Jr. Officials confirmed his title to the island in 1829, which officially had 1,781.53 acres.

Zephaniah Kingsley Jr. (1765 – 1843), one of the owners of Drayton Island, was a slave owner who built the beautiful Kingsley Plantation on the northern tip of Fort George Island north of Jacksonville, Florida.

Born in Scotland and educated in America, Kingsley eventually became a wealthy businessman in the field of coffee production. He married Anna Madgigine Jai (c. 1793 – 1870), an African princess with whom he had four children. He freed her from slavery in 1811 and placed her in charge of his plantations.

Kingsley Plantation is well preserved today on Fort George Island.

In an article entitled "Zephaniah Kingsley, Nonconformist (1765 – 1843)" in *The Florida Historical Quarterly*, author Philip May wrote that "In a brief period, Kingsley acquired many of the beauty spots along the lower St. Johns river and its environs," including Drayton Island.

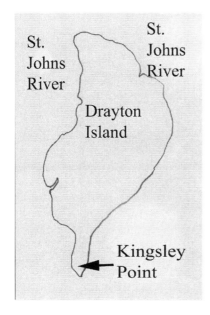

Although there is no proof that Kingsley ever visited Drayton Island, the southern tip of the island is named after him.

Kingsley must have had African-Americans on Drayton Island. In *The Weekly Standard* of Raleigh, North Carolina, for September 5, 1838 a report dated August 25, 1838, St. Augustine, said the following: "A Negro man belonging to Z. Kingsley, Esq. who was taken from Drayton's [sic.] Island, some time since by Indians, returned to town on Thursday evening last. He states that he was captured by the party, and carried to an island, which it took them six days to reach. He says that there are a large number of Indians, as he expresses it – 'plenty, plenty, plenty;' but as he is an old African, he has no very extended idea of numbers, and but little correct knowledge can be obtained from him. He can give no idea of the direction he travelled. He was six days in returning. He was dealt with hardly, and had but little food given him, which doubtless rendered him more anxious to effect his escape."

Apparently, Kingsley sought permission from officials to visit Drayton Island after he acquired it, but officials denied him permission, fearful that such a visit might antagonize the Seminole Indians in the vicinity.

Ten years after the United States acquired Florida from Spain as a result of the Adams–Onís Treaty of 1819, American officials confirmed Kingsley's ownership of Drayton Island.

Kingsley Point, which honors Zephaniah Kingsley Jr., used to have beaches and a swimming area for the island residents, but today the area has filled in with silt and trees, completely hiding the beaches.

According to the St. Johns County record deed book M, Zephaniah Kingsley sold Drayton Island to his son, George Kingsley, for $5,000 in 1836. Zephaniah died in New York City in 1843. His son George died in 1846 when the ship he was on from the Dominican Republic wrecked in a storm.

Various people then seemed to be interested in the island, and eventually, in 1851, Dr. John C. Calhoun Jr., son of the well-known late Senator Calhoun, bought the island for $3,968. He renamed the island Anzie Island after his wife: Angie "Anzie" Calhoun. Apparently, J.C. Calhoun Jr. had a house built in South Carolina and then shipped south by schooner to the island, where he had it installed.

His father, Senator John C. Calhoun (1782 – 1850), was a member of the House of Representatives and Senate, the seventh Vice President of the United States, and secretary of war and state. His son, John C. Calhoun Jr., died just four years after buying Drayton/Anzie Island and therefore probably did not get to spend much time there.

To the right is a picture of the grave site of Dr. John Caldwell Calhoun Jr. (1823 – 1855) in Pendleton, South Carolina.

In 1855, the island was sold at public auction in Palatka for $5,050 to Duff Green. Four years later, Duff Green and his wife, Laucretia Green, sold the island to Major William P. Rembert for $6,000.

Bad weather on the island in the 19th century

Drayton Island was subject to an occasional freeze, which did much harm to the agricultural crops grown there. For example, according to *Our Place in Time: A Chronology of Putnam County*, a disastrous freeze on February 8, 1835, saw temperatures dropping to eight degrees Fahrenheit. Ice covered all the vegetation and damaged century-old orange trees, including the orange grove that owner Zephaniah Kingsley Jr. had developed. Ice even formed along the shore line of the river.

The presence of such large woodpiles as can be seen on the island today indicates that freezes still occur there, although far fewer than for places north of there.

Possible involvement in the Seminole Indian Wars

As noted in *Our Place in Time: A Chronology of Putnam County*, in April, 1844, someone named Edward Anderson anchored off Drayton Island and wrote: "a block house built during the Indian war was the only habitation near by, save a Negro house on the premises."

The Indian wars referred to were probably either the First Seminole War (1816 – 1823) or the Second Seminole War (1835 – 1842). During those wars federal troops established outposts and forts in North and Central Florida, from which they could venture out to attack the Seminoles.

As an indication of how close the Seminole Indian Wars came to Drayton Island the *Democratic Free Press* (Detroit, Michigan) reported the following on July 12, 1837: "Three negroes belonging to Z. Kingsley, Esq., arrived at Picolata yesterday, from Drayton Island near Lake George, who report that they saw Indian fires all around them, and that they left home for fear of capture.

It is feared that the remainder, 17 in number, have been captured by the Indians, as they have not since been heard of. Mr. Kingsley re-established his plantation soon after the capitulation of the Indians."

The Evening Post (New York, New York), the *Charleston Courier,* and the *Jacksonville Courier* reported in July, 1837, that "Drayton Island has been abandoned by the whites, owing to the presence of Indians. It is also said that the Indians have burned the government buildings at Volusia."

The following year (May, 1838), *The Weekly Standard* (Raleigh, North Carolina) reported that *The St. Augustine Herald* wrote that "a large body of Indians visited Drayton's Island, and captured a number of negroes belonging to Z. Kingsley, Esq., and carried them to the west side of the St. John's River. The negroes effected their escape while the Indians were engaged in killing cattle, and came to Picolata. A negro woman was left on the Island and a steamboat passing by took her off. Fort Mellon is said to be abandoned, and also Fort Pierce. Troops are arriving here [in St. Augustine] daily from the South, on their way to the Cherokee nation."

Installations like Fort Christmas near Orlando were built during the Seminole Indian Wars to protect the soldiers who were fighting the Indians. Federal troops along the St. Johns River would have built similar forts, but probably smaller.

Other island news

The Evening Post (New York, New York) in its November 15, 1844 issue reported that the *St. Augustine News* noted a shipment of 40,000 oranges down the St. Johns from Drayton Island. Freezes, however, would greatly curtail such crops in the future.

Other owners of the island

One of the major owners of land on Drayton Island in the mid-nineteenth century was Major William Rembert, who bought the island from Duff Green in 1859 for $6,000 and then subdivided the island into five sections. The section at the northeast corner, which had about 552 acres and was called The Homestead, was where previous island owner J.C. Calhoun Jr. built his house.

The Civil War on Drayton Island

Although records are scarce for any Civil War events on the island, historian Edward Mueller mentions one in his book entitled *St. Johns River Steamboats* (p. 48). Three Union vessels, *Columbine*, *General Sumter*, and *Hattie*, were patrolling the St. Johns River near Drayton Island in May, 1864, when Union soldiers captured the son of Major Rembert of Drayton Island.

The young man, an officer in the Confederate army, convinced the federal troops that eighty Confederate soldiers were waiting to ambush the Union forces at Fort Gates north of the island. The crews of the Union vessels placed bales of cotton to work as barricades against what the crews expected to be an ambush, but nothing occurred when the boats passed Fort Gates.

The picture shows the capture of the Columbine *by Confederate troops on the St. Johns River on May 23, 1864.*

Developer R.W. Towle

Mr. R.W. Towle was an important builder/developer on the island in the 1870s. *The Clarksville Weekly Chronicle* of Clarksville, Tennessee, noted in its issue of June 12, 1875, that Mr. Towle in 1872 went south to Lake George with one thousand dollars to invest. He bought a small orange grove near the lake, grafted and sold his produce, built a small cottage of eight rooms, and sent his family to New York each summer, probably to escape the heat.

Later in 1875, he sold his fifteen acres for $7,000 in cash and then bought 250 acres on Drayton Island. The relatively frost-free island, which was serviced by daily steamers, was good for growing crops. Towle brought along much lumber to build a house and wharf, took along six African-American workers, and had the county surveyor survey his land into ten-acre lots. Before the survey was even finished, Mr. and Mrs. Alvord of Bridgeport, Connecticut, stopped by on the island and bought fifteen acres of wild-orange land from Towle for $1,500.

One of the structures that Towle built was the Towle Hotel, which later burned down. To the right is a picture of that hotel.

Towle's survey of the island

The fact that R.W. Towle had a county surveyor survey the land he bought on the island into ten-acre lots would be very important in future transactions on the island.

The Palatka Daily News, April 11, 1885, printed a long article entitled "In the Circuit Court" which dealt with the different surveys of the island:

"For some years disputes about the difference between two surveys have kept good neighbors at loggerheads on Drayton Island. This state of affairs has culminated in a variety of suits and Drayton Island has occupied a prominent place on the docket for several terms.

Now a decision has been rendered which settles practically these disputes until the matter is finally decided by our Supreme Court. The special case was Valentine L. Lombard vs. Wm. F. Reed. Ejectment – verdict for plaintiff.

So that Towle's survey now stands as authority for boundary lines on the east side of the Island. Messrs. Fleming and Daniel, through Frank P. Fleming, Esq., represented the plaintiff, while Messrs. Calhoun, Gillis & Calhoun presented the case of the victors."

Those who would buy land in that part of the island in the future would have to pay attention to Towle's survey.

A description of the Towle property

Although a description of the Towle site is rarely found, the *Nevada State Journal* (Reno, Nevada) for February 27, 1876, did have one:

"As an illustration of the change taking place around us, I will mention the case of a neighbor who bought a large tract of wild hammock land on Drayton Island ... and eight months ago commenced the task of clearing the land and erecting a hotel. Plenty of help was employed, and to-day we visited the place for the first time.

It seemed almost impossible to realize the great improvement which had been made. Though many of the natural beauties of the place still remained, yet a fine hotel, handsomely furnished, stood where a year ago the hunter roamed for deer.

Two houses already finished, and another in progress of construction, were near by, and many smaller buildings were scattered about. The white buildings, with green blinds, made a very pretty picture, clustered among the tall trees, with their swinging moss and graceful vines.

Near the hotel was a vegetable garden, showing cabbages the size of a water-pail."

The Palatka Daily News, August 20, 1884, noted the death of Richard Towle in Chicago. After a fire, Towle had gone to Palatka and then to Chicago, where he died.

More owners of the island

Towle took what was called the Towle Subdivision and further divided it into twenty-eight lots. Major Rembert and his wife, Satilla Rembert, sold a lot of a little over 405 acres on the island for $6,000 in 1872 to Wm. P. Wright. That piece included Cape Kingsley in the far south. They later sold another lot of a little more than 265 acres for around $4,000.

Three years later the Remberts sold 242 acres of the island to R.W. Towle for $4,000. In that same year the Remberts sold to Caroline Kirby a piece now called North Point, which consisted of 295 acres, for $5,000. All told then, Major Rembert bought the island for $6,000 and then sold much of it off in pieces for a total of $19,000, while keeping the main homestead of 552 acres and a large house.

The island's docks that extend out into the river today are reminiscent of the long docks that accommodated passing boats in the nineteenth century.

Steamboats calling at Drayton Island

Until the building of the railroad in Florida in the nineteenth century, steamboats plied the waters of the main rivers in the state, especially the major north – south artery: the St. Johns. The steamboats allowed farmers along the river to transport their products north to Jacksonville and markets elsewhere by means of ocean-going ships.

The picture here from the Florida State Archives is of the type of steamboats that went up and down the St. Johns and sometimes docked at Georgetown on the mainland and at one of several landing sites on the island, for example where Grampp's dock is today and two others south of there.
This picture shows the Kissimmee
at Fullers Wharf in Ellenton, Florida, in 1887.
This particular steamboat travelled on the St. Johns River and later on the Manatee River – Tampa run, before workers dismantled it in 1896.

Steamboats went between Jacksonville and Sanford below Lake George, stopping along the way to pick up cargo and passengers. As noted in *Our Place in Time: A Chronology of Putnam County,* in 1878 steamboats sometimes stopped at the island: "There are every day excursions to Drayton Island on steamers *Water Lily* and *Pastime.* Leaving Palatka at 8 a.m. and leaving the Island at 2:30 p.m. on the return. This is a most delightful trip and may be taken every day in the week, Sundays excepted. Round trip $2.00."

The distance on the river between Jacksonville and Drayton Island is about one hundred miles.

More newspaper notices about steamboats to Drayton Island

The Palatka Daily News, June 14, 1884, mentioned that the steamboat *Augusta* would be making daily trips round trip between Palatka and Drayton Island. The same newspaper, July 25, 1885, mentioned that the steamboat *Geo. M. Bird*, which had been running on the route between Palatka and Drayton Island for the past few months, was withdrawn from service, but that the steamers *Anita* and *Water Lily* "will take the freight for points on the river." (See image of *Anita* below.)

*A sketch of one of the many
steamboats on the St. Johns River*

The Palatka Daily News, January 5, 1887, noted that an "elegant little steam yacht, *Silver Star*, belonging to Capt. Barbour," would be running on the river between Palatka and Drayton Island. The vessel was 85 feet long and 20 feet broad, and the ladies' cabin was fitted up in elegant style in hard wood, with Brussels carpet. The freight capacity was from 500 – 700 boxes of oranges.

Reporters for *The Palatka Daily News* in the last part of the nineteenth century described idyllic trips along the St. Johns, including south from Palatka to Sanford on Lake Monroe. Some of the excursions called at Drayton Island, which often received high praise from the passengers on the steamboats, as well as from the reporters.

For example, that newspaper in its January 20, 1887 edition had an article about a trip from Palatka to Drayton Island, including these words: "From Palatka to Drayton Island the scenery is typical of our section; the groves are still laden with their luscious crop; every wharf is plied [piled high?] with boxes of fruits and barrels of vegetables, and on her return trip the decks of the boat are heaped with evidences, palpable to all our senses, in proof that even if our peninsula is a 'sand-bank,' its products are sought for everywhere.

And the passengers prove too that nowhere on earth can be found a better class of settlers, more healthy and well-to-do than those who honor the banks of our peerless river.

Here few visitors fail to find a Floridian who came originally from the State claimed by them as home; here the evidences of prosperity are better shown than they could be in any fair.

The sun is beaming overhead, the banks are graced alternately by grove and garden, within which are set the pretty homes of our people, and in the intervals still lie the primeval forests which await mournfully the day of doom now surely imminent.

Thus we sail on between the evidences of a high civilization and the still living show of what remains to do, and the air quivers with a midwinter warmth only found in Florida, and soft waves ripple around the bow of our steamer; then gradually the daylight dies as we push, with a shrill whistle, into the flashing waves of Lake George and tie up at Drayton Island.

Here again the towering pines and spreading oaks, which once sheltered the quiet retreats of the rulers of our forests, have given place to the orange and the home of the civilized man; where the king of Florida's first owners ruled his tawny warriors, now live those who speak a language brought from across the seas, and claim birth with pride from Maine and Massachusetts, the wide prairies of the West and the rich rocks and mines of California, Pennsylvania and Alabama."

Such high praise must have drawn even more visitors and settlers to the island.

Praise for Drayton Island in a Rochester, NY, newspaper

The Democrat and Chronicle newspaper out of Rochester for March 14, 1886 (p. 4) had a long column from a correspondent, L.M. Wilson, that was full of praise for the Florida island. Excerpts are as follows: "About two months ago I left Batavia in quest of a climate free from blizzards and mountains of snow. Such a place I found on Drayton Island....

The everlasting Florida moss transforms [the trees there] into veritable Rip Van Winkles in appearance, hanging as it does from almost every tree and branch in long swaying masses or graceful festoons of gray.

The best water for drinking and cooking is rain water, and strange to say, the more it is exposed to the air and shade the cooler it is, and the deeper you go for it the warmer it is and the more sulphur you get.

As I look out of the window I can see the jassamine clothed with the blossoms of yellow, climbing the trunks and hanging from the branches of the cypress and the Magnolia. Birds of every hue are warbling in the forests....

Every man has a row boat, instead of a carriage and many is the merry crew I have seen passing our front on some fishing, gunning or other pleasure excursion, composed more or less of northerners who are here in abundance from almost every state in the union."

The long newspaper column was effusive in its praise for Drayton Island. One wonders how many fellow New Yorkers the writer was able to convince to make the trek south to the idyllic island at the head of Lake George.

Drayton Island in the last part of the nineteenth century

As noted in *Our Place in Time: A Chronology of Putnam County* the postmaster on the island in 1875 was D.W. Crosby, and the post office was a quarter of a mile from the steamboat landing. The post office served fifty residents.

According to the same book, the population of the island in 1889 was 150, and land was selling for $100 – $300 an acre. The soil, which consisted of dark sandy loam, continued to be good for growing fruits and vegetables.

At that time (around 1889) Samuel Parker was the postmaster, B.M. Pettit was the physician, and orange growers or merchants included Daniel Darling & Son, V.L. Lomboard & Son, D. Pullon, W.F. Reed, H.D. Rehberg, and W.P. Wright.

By 1895, there were 60 people on the island, and it had a post office, S. Parker and Dr. Pellet boarding houses. It also had nine orange growers and two fruit and vegetable growers and shippers.

This image from the late 1800s shows some men camping near Lake George.

Problems with growing melons on the island
and shipping them north

The Palatka Daily News for October 22, 1886, pointed out the real hardship of growing melons on Drayton Island and then shipping them north. In June of 1886, Mr. W.P. Wright shipped 901 melons to New York City for sale. When the melons reached New York, the shipping charges were so high that Mr. Wright received nothing for them. The freight company, in fact, sold the melons to cover the freight charges.

The newspaper editor advised growers like Mr. Wright to avoid sending more melons north at that time because of the excessive charges that the freight companies had for such shipments. Instead, the editor suggested, the melon growers should switch to growing corn, then feed the corn to local pigs, later kill the pigs in the early winter, and store the carcasses for local consumption. The editor concluded: "This is the way to make money out of a melon patch, and get even with transportation lines."

Mr. Wright, who had sixteen years' experience at that point in the growing of crops, had fifty acres of oranges growing on the island, as well as five acres of Irish potatoes and fifteen acres of cucumbers, Other growers on the island at that time were Samuel Parker (who had five – six acres in potatoes and cabbages), Dr. J.J. Pettitt (who had some five hundred barrels of cabbages to send to market), and – at Mount Royal – Mr. Frank Wright (who had some ten acres of cucumbers, potatoes, and squashes).

The issue of what kind of crop to grow on Drayton Island and how growers should send them to markets elsewhere was a very important one for all concerned. Only when transportation costs became more reasonable with steamships or the railroad would growers see the profit they rightly deserved.

Until freezes finally forced orange growers on the island and in the vicinity to give up and head south, many farmers had prospered with the growing of crops, including citrus. One of the brands shipped from the island was Gale's Drayton Island Brand.

The label here is from the
University of Florida archival collection.

Orange growing and packing on the island

Charles Mooney's *Soil Survey of Putnam County, Florida* noted that the best places to grow crops, including oranges, was along the southern and eastern parts of the island for two reasons.

First, the cold winds that could harm the crops tend to come from the north. Secondly, before the cold air hits the crops, it has to pass over water, i.e. the St. Johns River, and such cold air then becomes less cold.

That must have been why the growers of oranges had large groves in the southern part of the island, as evidenced by the dilapidated orange-packing warehouse there. (See photo below.)

Until freezes finally drove away the orange growers, they made a good living growing large, lucrative crops of citrus. They also had packing houses, from which they shipped their product north via steamers that could dock at long piers that stretched into the St. Johns.

But once the freezes stopped the citrus production, the packers moved, forcing the farmers once again to adapt to the circumstances and switch to other crops.

Excursions from the island

Occasionally the island residents would take a steamer/ railroad excursion to other towns.

For example, *The Palatka Daily News* for April 15, 1887, noted that the residents could take a ride on the steamer *Georgea* and the St. Johns and Halifax Railroad to Daytona on the coast for a round-trip fare of $1.25.

*The St. Johns and Halifax
Railroad ran to Daytona.*

Georgetown in the last half of the nineteenth century

Nearby Georgetown had mail delivered to it for the settlement of Lake George, which was two miles south of Georgetown and whose post office was discontinued twice: in 1860 and in 1888. In 1878, Georgetown had a box factory, packing house, and 36 groves with over 9,000 trees and another 2,680 in nursery farms.

A newspaper piece from *The Wyandott Herald* of Kansas City, Kansas, February 7, 1878, page 2, describes little Georgetown in very picturesque terms: "Georgetown is a busy little place – that is, for Florida. It has two wharves, a sawmill (steam), a store, post office, and a Justice of the Peace. There is also a school house, and a hardshell Baptist holds forth therein the third Sunday in each month.

There is no saloon. The store keeper sells whiskey among other necessaries (?), but does not allow it drank [sic] on his premises. An intoxicated individual calling for more liquor once, was refused.

He became abusive, and threatened to help himself to the same, whereupon the urbane merchant remonstrated with him so effectually with his revolver that the would-be imbiber lay for weeks in mortal bodily peril, and after recovery was heard devoutly to remark that he 'reckoned that shopkeeper most ginerally [sic] meant what he said.' I think the community, generally, are of the same opinion."

Georgetown in 1884

By 1884, the town had a daily packet boat service to and from Palatka, as well as a daily mail boat. Three other steamboats called there three times a week. A.B. Bartlett was a lawyer, A.A. Stewart was clerk of the county court, and general-merchandise stores were operated by Burchsted & Thorn and R.A. Labree & Co. Workers included carpenters Orin LaBree and Edwin Tappen, while D.V. Causey was a cooper, William Perry was a cabinet maker, and Philip Stephens was a painter. Also George H. Thorn was the express agent, Aaron Warr was a shoemaker, and David Vandergriff was involved with fishing.

Thomas Hind of Georgetown represented Putnam County in the Florida House. In 1888 – 1890, he was elected to the Florida Senate. In 1895, Georgetown had a population of 50, a money-order post office, churches, and 45 students in schools. Residents still had to go to Palatka, which was 35 miles away, for bank services.

Old, weathered houses like this one in Georgetown on the mainland may have been part of a boat-building operation years ago.

*Paddle steamer "Chattahoochee" moored at dock
on the Saint Johns River near Georgetown*

Another picture of the "Chattahoochee" on the St. Johns in the 1890s

Fire in 1878

The *News-Herald* from Hillsboro, Ohio, for November 17, 1898, mentioned that the distinguished writer, William Armstrong Collins, died in Maryland. In 1874, he had gone to Virginia and then Florida, where he established a large orange plantation on Drayton Island and built what was called "a handsome home." In 1878, fire destroyed that residence, along with the manuscripts and personal property of Mr. Collins. He then moved away to St. Augustine and then to Hagerstown, Maryland.

High praise in 1878 from a Kansas newspaper

A newspaper piece from *The Wyandott Herald* of Kansas City, Kansas, February 7, 1878, page 2, mentions a tree on Drayton Island in very positive terms: "The crowning beauty of Drayton Island …is a real date-palm, looking exactly like the pictures of the same in geographies and books of travel.

The date-palm on the island may have resembled this impressive one.

The underbrush, however, is so dense, and the tree so lofty that the dates cannot be gathered in their prime, but only when they fall – so ripe that they leave the seeds behind them, and themselves are withered…. The soil is very fertile on the island, and it is so surrounded with water that frosts do not trouble it, as they do both shores of the river, and the west bank more than the eastern."

The writer concludes with much praise for the island: "Steamboats pass up and down, sail boats and row boats skim by, tree-toads sing all night, sounding like distant sleigh bells, days and nights glide past, monotonously, and time almost himself seems to stand still."

Although the date-palm mentioned in the article may be hard to identify, residents do point out with pride another immense tree near some of the island's houses. Below is a picture of that very large tree.

The island still has a good variety of trees, including remnants of the thousands of citrus trees, especially in the former orange groves near the southern end of the island.

One can also see the occasional citrus tree today on property around the island, but the freezes of a hundred-plus years ago effectively ended the commercial growing of citrus on the island.

1880 census of the people that lived on
Drayton Island in the 1870s

NAME, AGE, OCCUPATION, STATE OF BIRTH

Peters, Henry W., 57, Physician, Ky.
Peters, Bell C., 36, Wife, Ky.
Peters, Henry W., 12, Son, Ark.
Alvoid, Nelson, 50, Retired merchant, Conn.
Beckham, Herman, 46, Servant, N.C.
Reed, William F., 25, Servant, R.I.

Crosby, Daniel W., 49, Fruit grower, Me.
Crosby, Ellen H., 39, Wife, Mass.
Thomas, Cherry, 30, Servant, Fla.
White, William, 28, Servant, Ga.
Beemus, Julius, 22, Servant, Fla.
Jones, Julius, 22, Servant, Fla.
Filken, J.A., 44, Carpenter, N.Y.
Filken, S.A., 21, Carpenter, NY

Rogers, J. Thomas, 31, Farmer, Me.

Darling, Daniel, 52, Farmer, Vt.
Darling, Francis, 36, Wife, N.J.
Darling, George, 20, Son (in school), Mass.
Darling, Lydia A., 16, Daughter (in school), Mass.
Fry, Viola, M.A., 10, Boarder (in school), N.Y.

Wright, W. Pelham, 35, Truck gardener, N.Y.
McLain, Jesse, 25, Servant, Fla.
Bradley, Samuel, 23, Servant, Fla.

[continued on next page]

[1880 census continued from previous page]

Sinkers, Baze, 38, Servant, Fla.
Sinkers, Milly, 28, Servant, Fla.
Sinkers, George, 5, Servant, Fla.
Sinkers, Daniel W., 2, Servant, Fla.
Johnson, James, 10, Servant, Fla.

Pullen, Duane, 33, Farmer, N.J.

Rembert, Satilla, 49, Farmer, Ga.
Rembert, Waddilla, 14, Son (in school), Ga.
Rembert, Turissa, 8, Daughter (in school), Ga.
Walker, Henry, 29, Servant, Fla.
Bogart, George W., 50, Tenant, Fla.

Sodock, Edward, 28, Servant, Fla.

Scurry, Samual, 35, Truck gardener, Va.
Scurry, Louise, 40, Wife, Va.
Sloan, Ellen, 19, Daughter, Va.
Scurry, Betsy, 18, Sister, Va.

Mixer, Albert, 35, Truck gardener, N.Y.
Small, Sual, 66, Truck gardener, N.Y.
Cooper, Thomas, 34, Truck gardener, N.Y.

Manville, R.E., 23, Nurseryman, Ill.
Manville, Ellen, 49, Keeping House, N.Y.
Hughes, Maime, 16, In school, Tenn.
Hughes, Freddie, 12, In school, Tenn.
Griffin, Martin, 39, Banker, ?
Griffin, Sarah, 36, Wife, N.Y.
Manuel, Nathan, 43, Servant, Fla.

Other island news

Fishing could be very good around the island. *The News and Observer* newspaper of Raleigh, North Carolina, mentioned on October 27, 1881, that "Frank Lebo caught 275 mullet from 7 to 10 o'clock near Drayton Island, Florida, with a small net."

In 1882, Rev. A.A. Presbrey excavated and shipped thirteen tons of marl from a deposit on his lands on Drayton Island. Marl is a calcium carbonate or lime-rich mud that contains clay and silt.

The Tennessean (Nashville, Tennessee) on January 11, 1884, noted that "Drayton Island Marl is a new Florida production." Also two years earlier, in 1882, *The People's Press* (Winston-Salem, North Carolina) reported that "Orange, lemon and lime trees are in blossom, roses abundant and vegetables plenty on Drayton Island, Florida."

A long-time resident that lives near the island

More postal news on the island

The Palatka Daily News (April 6, 1886) noted that "The postmaster general has ordered that a contract be made with Beach & Miller, of Crescent City, for conveying the mail on route No. 16,080, from Palatka to Drayton Island and back, six times a week, from April 16th to June 30th, 1886, inclusive.

The mails will be delivered by the postmaster here accordingly. The contract price is at the rate of $2,000 per annum." The article concludes with the announcement that several other postal routes from Palatka to Enterprise will be discontinued. Sam'l [Samuel?] Parker was named postmaster for Drayton Island in 1889.

Residents found this skeleton and carcass of a very large gator on the island.

Potato growing in Putnam County, including Drayton Island

When orange growers gave up because of the hard freezes that hit the island (and the rest of North Florida), some of the farmers turned to the growing of potatoes. According to Charles Mooney's *Soil Survey of Putnam County, Florida*, the Florida farmers found that they had a distinct advantage over potato growers in other parts of the United States because the Florida growers grew the potatoes in the winter, unlike growers elsewhere.

Therefore when the growers, for example from Putnam County (where Drayton Island is located) were able to ship their potato crops to northern markets, they found that they could earn higher prices since growers elsewhere were not able to ship their products so early.

One problem with the growing of crops like potatoes in Putnam County was that the crops grown there were hurt by flooding from the St. Johns River. The growers built ditches on their land to drain the excess water away from their crops. One can still see such ditches on Drayton Island today as in the picture below.

Ditches could also drain water away from the main road that runs down the center of the island. Many residents, especially those without easy access to boats, relied on that main road, which they would use from the ferry on the northern tip to their own property.

The agricultural history of the island
in the nineteenth century

The 1916 publication of Charles Mooney's *Soil Survey of Putnam County, Florida* (see Bibliography) outlined the nineteenth century's agricultural history of the island:

1.   From the time of the earliest pioneer white settlers in the early 1850s, agriculture was secondary to hunting and fishing for sustenance.

2.   Through the 1850s cotton growing became somewhat important, but it relied on slave labor. The Civil War (1861 to 1865) ended the practice of slavery and the cotton industry in all of Florida, including Putnam County.

3.   From the end of the Civil War to the late 1870s, agriculture became more diversified as farmers planted a variety of crops.

4.   The fourth period began in the mid-1870s and emphasized the growing of citrus. By 1890, that industry replaced the others. The best locations for the planting and harvesting of citrus was near bodies of water, including lakes and rivers. That factor would be important for those farmers on Drayton Island.

5.   The fifth period began in the terrible winter of 1894 – 1895, when the so-called "great freeze" killed many, if not most of the orange trees in the county. Because growers had confined themselves to just growing citrus, the demise of that industry led to financial ruin for growers, many of whom abandoned their fields. Those who tried to revive the orange industry were hit by a severe freeze two years later (1897 – 1898), followed by another one in 1899. Some farmers switched to turpentining and then lumbering or – in some cases – the growing of potatoes and corn.

Chapter Seven: Twentieth Century

1900 - 1909

The population of Drayton Island in 1900 was 20. That number would not increase dramatically for the rest of the century. The population of Georgetown across the channel was 50 in 1900. By 1906, the population of the town had increased to 125. The businesses included a turpentine facility, a lumber company, and a general store.

In the early 1900s, the postmaster of the post office on the island was J.C. Rogers; mail was delivered daily, at least during the week. J.T. Rogers had a general store on the island. By 1911, the postmaster was D.F. Pollock.

The Ocklawaha River Ferry, pictured here around 1902, may have been similar to a ferry that serviced Drayton Island.

Murder on Drayton Island

The island had relatively few crimes, but, according to *The Palatka News*, April 19, 1907, it saw a murder: Adolphus Kimball shot and killed Jim Way near the steamer landing at Drayton Island. The two men were arguing in a house belonging to Kimball, when the argument escalated to a fight in which Kimball got a rifle and shot and killed Way.

The county authorities were notified, Coroner Rowton – with a jury – went to the scene of the tragedy, and investigated the case, after which the jury rendered a verdict of justifiable homicide.

1910 - 1919

Forest fires

From time to time, the island suffered damages from forest fires. For example, in June, 1910, a bad fire swept across the southeastern side of the island, pushed on by a strong gale coming from the west.

It finally stopped at the water's edge on the eastern shore, but not before heavily damaging three unoccupied houses and two packing houses.

Island creatures like this bald eagle were affected by fires there.

Douglass Fish Camp on Lake George near Georgetown around 1917

Around 1911, D.F. Pollock (who was also the postmaster then) had a general store, W.F. Reed had a nursery, and the orange growers were the McCaskill Brothers and C.B. Pettitt. The population of Georgetown across the river was 125, although that decreased to 100 in 1918.

*A postmark from 1912 that has
the name of Drayton Island*

Tragic shooting near Drayton Island

The Palatka News and Advertiser, September 29, 1911, had the details of a tragic shooting near the island that year. When Sheriff Smith of Volusia was on Lake George looking for persons engaged in illegal fishing, he spotted two brothers from Drayton Island, W.A. and Allen McCaskill, two independent fishermen, out in their boat.

When the sheriff stopped the two brothers and told them that he was going to arrest them, they asked him if he had a warrant. When he replied in the negative, the brothers told him that they lived on Drayton Island and could be found there when the sheriff obtained a warrant.

They then continued on their way home.

For some reason, as the brothers were heading home, Sheriff Smith shot at them, fatally wounding W.A. McCaskill. The sheriff claimed that he had ordered the brothers' boat to stop, but the sound of the boat's engine may have prevented them from hearing the order.

The sheriff claimed that he intended to fire a shot over the brothers' boat, but that another party in the sheriff's boat lurched against the sheriff and caused the bullet to go lower than originally planned – with the result that it struck McCaskill in the head.

The dead man, W.A. McCaskill, was the youngest of three brothers who had migrated to the area from Alabama around 1875. He was married around 1904 to Miss Theresa Rembert, and they had one child one or two years old.

The dead man was apparently buried on Drayton Island, but his son may have been buried at the Georgetown Cemetery when he died in 1965. The photo here may be of the grave site of the murdered man's child.

Steamboats serving Drayton Island

In 1917, the vessel *Alma May* was launched to begin a Palatka – Drayton Island mail run. The boat was captained by R.I. Allen. According to the State Archives in Tallahassee, the vessel pictured below may have been the *Alma May*.

Other island news

The Palatka News and Advertiser, July 6, 1917, named these people from Drayton Island whose registration cards were on file in the Palatka office, probably for World War I: Williams Dilworth, Oscar Moore, & S.J. Nelson.

The Sandusky Star-Journal (Sandusky, Ohio) reported on November 12, 1919, that Herman Rehberg and his wife spent winters on Drayton Island.

1920 - 1929

Martin Wendel was the postmaster on Drayton Island in 1922. People interviewed on the island in the research for this book had much to say about Mr. Wendel, as one who helped women give birth to children in the area, brewed wine in his living room, and collected eels and rattlesnakes on the island to ship north on steamboats. He apparently lived in the house next to the Grampp house until he died in his nineties.

The population of nearby Georgetown in 1925 was 200. That year, according to *Our Place in Time: A Chronology of Putnam County*, the famous Chinese-American horticulturist, Lu Gim Gong, had left most of his estate and all of his personal belongings, including a formula for what he claimed was a cure for cancer, to Mrs. W.F. Reed of Georgetown. She had volunteered to work with Gong after the death of his business manager.

1930 - 1939

Residents of Drayton Island, realizing that a ferry would provide necessary transportation between the island and Georgetown on the mainland petitioned officials for a ferry. They would have to wait four years for the ferry to be operational.

A church in Georgetown today

Marjorie Kinnan Rawlings and Drayton Island

One of the most famous twentieth-century Florida authors who mentioned Drayton Island was Marjorie Kinnan Rawlings (1896 – 1953), author of *The Yearling, Cross Creek, South Moon Under*, and many short stories about the Scrub of north-central Florida. When she divorced Charles Rawlings in 1933 and was feeling somewhat depressed, her friend Dessie invited her to travel down the St. Johns River, camping along the way and experiencing the wilds of Florida.

Marjorie Kinnan Rawlings at her typewriter
in her home at Cross Creek, Florida

They had some memorable experiences, including a harrowing trip across Lake George until they reached the safety of Georgetown at the northern tip of what she called "Drayton's Island." They were glad to end their journey at the Ocklawaha River north of there, but the river played a major part in the last chapter in *Cross Creek*, a chapter she entitled "Hyacinth Drift."

*The photo above shows co-author Walt Grampp
with a male neighbor
by the river in the early 1930s;
the trees and road behind them are gone.
The male neighbor may have been one of the priests
from the upper Midwest who rented the house
next to the Grampps.*

1940 - 1949
Drayton Island Ferry

For those who do not have their own boats, the ferry that goes to the island from the mainland just west of Georgetown is essential. Similar to the Fort Gates Ferry to the north of the site, the Drayton Island Ferry began operating in 1943.

An early ferry to and from the island

Four years after the island residents petitioned county officials for a ferry in 1939, the operation began. The first vessel sank in an accident in 1956 and was salvaged, but was then replaced by a boat that was 48 feet long and 18 feet wide at a cost of over $6,700. The passenger limit was set at six people, but reports surfaced from time to time that the ferry carried many more than that. In the 1960s, the ferry collected over $2,200 in tolls, but also relied on a yearly county subsidy of $1,800 to operate.

Other island news

The island attracted a number of priests who went there for vacation or recuperation. For example, *The Post-Crescent* (Appleton, Wisconsin) on January 22, 1940, reported that the Rev. H.E. Hunck, pastor of St. Mary's Church in Chilton, Wisconsin, was going to "travel by train to Drayton Island where he will spend his time fishing and recuperating from his recent illness until sometime in March."

Former dock on the island

This aerial view of a dock off the Grampp property shows a boathouse at the end and boats tied up to the dock. A hurricane eventually destroyed the boathouse, but – until that point – the dock provided mooring for a number of boats belonging to owners on the island.

1950 - 1959

When an old barge sank carrying two trucks loaded with fruit around 1956, the Putnam County commissioners authorized a call for bids for a new 40-ton barge to take vehicles between Georgetown and Drayton Island. Officials were able to salvage the original ferry barge and return it to service, but they later bought a replacement that measured 48 feet long and 18 feet wide from J.H. Coppedge and Co. in Jacksonville for $6,793.

A newspaper article in the *Lawton Constitution* in Lawton, Oklahoma, on June 9, 1957, p. 1, indicated that a twister "cut a 150-foot wide swath across Drayton Island in the St. Johns River south of Palatka." It gave no indication about any fatalities.

Homeowners have been building bulkheads at the edge of their property for many years. Weeds and growth from the river have inched closer to the homes. (See next page for more about the problem of hyacinths.)

1960 - 1969

In 1963, officials tried to limit the number of passengers on the ferry between Drayton Island and Georgetown to six, but sometimes with only limited success. In 1967, the operation of the ferry cost the county $4,129. Toll revenues in the mid-1960s were $2,267.

The 1960s saw a major spreading of hyacinths, something that has bothered waterfront owners on Drayton Island since then. The floating weeds can clog up vast areas of lakes and rivers, as well as propellers on boats. First introduced into the St. Johns, possibly in Palatka, the hyacinths spread very rapidly and covered at one time 120,000 acres of public lakes and navigable rivers by the 1960s.

Workers from the Florida Fish and Wildlife Commission sprayed hyacinth fields in the 1960s and 1970s.

*The boathouse at the end of the Grampp dock
was separated from the island after a storm.*

Hurricanes and other strong storms often damaged or wrecked the boathouses at the end of the docks on the island, forcing homeowners to construct much stronger structures. Boaters who go around the island can see some very sturdy boathouses and docks, the photos of which are presented throughout this book.

1970 - 1979

Mail delivery

The delivery of mail to the island has been an important issue in the last 150 years. One solution in the nineteenth century was to have regular service out of Palatka. *The Palatka Daily News* (April 6, 1886), for example, noted that "The postmaster general has ordered that a contract be made with Beach & Miller, of Crescent City, for conveying the mail on route No. 16,080, from Palatka to Drayton Island and back, six times a week, from April 16th to June 30th, 1886, inclusive. The mails will be delivered by the postmaster here accordingly. The contract price is at the rate of $2,000 per annum." The article concludes with the announcement that several other postal routes from Palatka to Enterprise will be discontinued.

In 1974, mail service to the island had a new carrier when Ruth Faircloth retired after working for the St. Johns waterway mail service for about thirty years. Before that, her husband, Captain Faircloth, had performed the service. In 1974, Ruth Faircloth's son-in-law, W.A. Jacobs, bid for and won the route. Then he and Ruth Jacobs continued delivering the mail to the island, something that had been passed down for two generations and, according to an article by Frank Hays (see Bibliography), was "the only one of its kind in Florida."

Mail boxes today are near the ferry landing.

95

1980 - 1989

Local officials proposed that repairs be made to the ferry landing in the early 1980s – to be paid for by a special taxing district, but the proposal was rejected as unneeded by the residents. Some islanders had raised questions about the financial management of the ferry operation at that time.

In 1986, Jr. [Junior?] Weldon captured a large gator, measuring 13' 5" and weighing 653 pounds. The young man caught the gator near the ferry to Drayton Island. Trappers took the gator to Nautilus Sports Medical Industries at Lake Helen, where scientists were breeding reptiles. Officials there planned to breed the gator in order to produce similar-sized reptiles.

Occasionally, large gators are found near the island. In 2001, gator hunters captured one near the island that was thirteen feet long and weighed almost 900 pounds. Two years later, hunters caught one off the west side of the island that was twelve feet, seven inches long.

Smaller gators like this one are often found near the river.

Other island news

In 1982, a seller was offering one acre on Drayton Island, "located amid the breathtaking splendor of Lake George in North Central Florida," for $8,000 or the best offer. (*The Palm Beach Post*, August 25, 1982)

One man, who was an assistant on the Drayton Island Ferry, used that experience to land a job as the pilot of the Fort Gates Ferry. *The Palm Beach Post* (West Palm Beach, Florida) for September 8, 1985, reported that Gary Price learned enough as a commercial fisherman and assistant on the Drayton Island Ferry to succeed as the Fort Gates Ferry operator. For the past year he had guided many passengers on his ferry through thunderstorms, freezes, steamy heat, and rough waters between Gateway Fish Camp on the east side of the river and the Ocala National Forest on the west side.

He was philosophical about his job: "Piloting a ferry is not an exact science, and there have been times when I've bumped the dock. There's no reverse on this boat, so you have to do it right going in. But when you carry people across, and it's real windy, and you bring it in nice and gentle, and they tell me I'm the best they've ever seen – that makes it all feel worthwhile."

This is a 1989 aerial photo of Drayton Island.

Ferry closings

When Florida Department of Transportation (DOT) officials inspected the loading ramps of the island ferry in late 1983, they found that the wooden supports beneath the ramp were rotted and shaky. Such inspections were part of the annual examination of the ramps on each side of the crossing (the mainland and the island) done by the DOT.

The ferry landing on the mainland side

Because the ferry and privately owned boats are the only way for island residents to go between the island and the mainland, those without access to boats were inconvenienced while the ferry was shut down.

Putnam County, which owns the ferry and its docking facilities, contracts with a private individual, like long-time ferry operator Eddie Babbitt Jr., to run the ferry. The operator was allowed to keep the fees charged to passengers and earned $700 a month from the county.

Among the arrangements made during the ferry closing were these: Lt. Col. Norris Sauls of Lake Como moved his fire truck to the island; the chief of the Georgetown Fire Department, Ed Albecker, secured boats, pumps, and hoses to be taken to the island for the purpose of fire fighting; the sheriff's department marine unit made itself available for law-enforcement duties on the island; the U.S. Forest Service and the state's Forestry Division made helicopters available to make water drops and to take personnel to the island; the U.S. Army Corps of Engineers made air boats available; and the U.S. Army Reserve made amphibious vessels available.

The ferry landing on the island side

The island residents knew they had to put up with such inconveniences from time to time, but it was a small price to pay for the chance to live on the island.

99

1990 - 1999

In March, 1991, a strong tornado hit Drayton Island as well as Georgetown and Lake Crescent Estates near Pomona Park. It caused damage estimated at between $750,000 and $1 million.

One of the persistent problems in Florida rivers, lakes, and back country for decades has been the poacher, the illegal hunter, the one who deliberately flouts the laws that most people obey. Bob Lee, a water patrol officer on the St. Johns River and a land patrol lieutenant in Putnam County, had many encounters with criminals in the last half of the twentieth century.

In his book entitled *Backcountry Lawman: True Stories from a Florida Game Warden*, officer Lee recounted true tales of trying to catch those who engage in "monkey fishing" (illegally catching fresh-water catfish using an electrical charge) on the St. Johns between Welaka and Georgetown across from Drayton Island.

Bob Lee's book is about illegal fishing and hunting on and near the St. Johns River in Putnam County.

Chapter Eight: Twenty-first Century

2000 - 2009

Fighting fires on the island

The threat of fire on the island has been a serious one since lightning or careless people can cause widespread fire damage. For a while the islanders had a decent fire engine, but its brakes did not work adequately, which led to a collision that disabled the machine. When authorities supplied the island with a modern fire engine, the authorities would not give the islanders its key since they believed that none of the islanders were certified by Florida fire-fighting officials. Actually, two of the islanders had been fire chiefs back in New Jersey, where they came from, and – in fact – one of the men had actually taught fire-fighting officials there how to fight fires.

The modern fire truck that never gets used

And so the fire engine sits idly in a garage on the island, ready to fight fires whenever the mainland authorities authorize the islanders to do so. In case of a fire, and fires have occurred from time to time, the local volunteers have to use bucket brigades to carry water to the scene or have to wait for fire fighters on the mainland to take their truck(s) on the ferry to the island and then maneuver them on the dirt road that runs down the middle of the island to the scene of the fire.

Church bell

Near the fire truck is an impressive bell that sits on its own pedestal. The bell comes from a manufacturing plant or locomotive in northern New Jersey where Walt Grampp's father had a tavern. Walt's father obtained the bell for a local church or house, perhaps in Georgetown across the channel. Someone would ring the bell on Sundays to invite people to go to the church. Finally, someone moved the bell to the island next to the garage that houses the idle fire engine. See picture below – with an arrow pointing to the bell.

Moving a house to the island

In January, 2003, professional movers loaded a 120-year-old house in Georgetown onto a ferry and carefully took it across the channel to its new home on the island. The house, which local residents estimate was built around 1880, had seen the birth of several local residents, including Eddie Babbitt Jr.

With signs in various local establishments announcing "a house-moving party," as many as five hundred people went down to the ferry dock to witness the move. It took two days to complete the move since the barge got stuck on a sandbar and had to be pushed off the next day. Workers very carefully moved the old house to the northwestern part of the island, where the owners have worked to restore it.

A tug boat carefully pushed the ferry with the house on it to the island.

Moving ornamental gators to the island

When a home owner in 2004 wanted to move some very large ornamental alligators to his property on the island, it took a great deal of coordination between the vendor and a local ferry service. The same is true for moving anything large to the island, for example kitchen appliances and large, bulky items.

Moving the gators by truck and ferry to the island

*One of the
ornamental gators
in place
on an island lawn*

Unwanted visitor on the island

Around 2004, island residents found a derelict boat at the edge of their island, just north of the ferry landing. With its stern wedged on the island, the bow extended into the river and slowly deteriorated as wave and wind action took their toll on the old vessel. When the man who owned the boat died, his widow tried to sell the boat, but had no takers.

The boat that no one wanted

Eventually a storm broke the boat in two and sank much of it into the water. The U.S. Coast Guard threatened to fine the widow for each day that she allowed the boat to remain where it was, especially because fuel was leaking from the fuel tanks.

Finally a group of investors bought the land on which part of the boat rested and received a grant to remove the boat, which they did.

2010 - 2016

Edward E. "Eddie" Babbitt Jr.

On January 6, 2013, Edward E. "Eddie" Babbitt Jr. died at the age of 82 at Putnam Community Medical Center in Palatka after a long illness. Known by many in the area as the "Mayor of Georgetown," Eddie was born in the small town of Georgetown and lived there most of his life.

He graduated from Crescent City High School in 1948 and then left Georgetown to join the U.S. Army to serve his country during the Korean Conflict – one of the few times he ever left the area. Although he worked as an electrical contractor, he was best known as the one who operated the Drayton Island Ferry for many years. He also served as president of the Georgetown – Fruitland Volunteer Fire Department. He is buried in the Georgetown Cemetery.

The first operator of the ferry was supposedly Billy Babbitt, Eddie's father. Eddie himself later took over its operation and is honored in the naming of the landing on the mainland. The sign indicates that Eddie operated the ferry from 1972 to 2009. The ferry has variable hours.

Babbitt with a visitor from England on the ferry

Houses on the island

As examples of the different kinds of houses on the island, here are four.

An old-two storey house that has been added onto

A house with a cistern near its fence

An idyllic cottage near the river

A relatively new house meant to withstand hurricanes

More sights around Drayton Island
Tour bus

One unexpected sight today is a bus with the words "Drayton Island Tours" painted on its side. Apparently, one of the local residents bought the bus a number of years ago, actually traveled in it to Alaska with others, brought it back, transported it to the island, and offered tours to friends.

After the bus had outlived its usefulness, it was abandoned in the bushes – probably never to be used again.

The bus that gave Drayton Island tours

Propeller

Another unexpected sight is of a large propeller near the water's edge. While one might guess that it comes from a very large ship, maybe one that was abandoned in the area, in fact it comes from the Miami River area in South Florida.

A local resident on Drayton Island worked in salvage down near Miami and brought the propeller to the island as a memento of his former business.

Cannon

The fairly innocuous-looking piece of oval metal lying by the side of the river/lake is actually a cannon that, when fired, tells everyone on the island that it's "party time." Usually around New Year's Eve or New Year's Day, the owner of the cannon yells "fire in the hole" or something like that, then lights the cannon, and runs for cover.

When island residents hear the boom, they know they are to bring food and join their neighbors for an afternoon of good camaraderie. So important are such gatherings that the normally friendly neighbors have been known to exclude those whom they consider cantankerous and therefore not welcome.

Steam shovel and bucket

The large steam shovel and its nearby bucket go back to a time years ago when one of the land-owners brought over the very heavy structure to build an embank-ment between his property and the river/lake. He picked a quiet day to have the ferry bring over the shovel, landed it on Drayton Island, and then "walked" it slowly and care-fully down the main road to his property.

The move took a long four-teen hours in order to make sure that there were no acci-dents. So there the two mementoes of the whole opera-tion sit.

Name post

There is at least one tall post along the main road that lists the names of the residents or home owners who live down the road that branches off that main road.

Necessity of having a boat on the island

Many residents on the island have a boat of their own, not only to fish and take excursions, but – more importantly – to go

between the island and the mainland without relying on the ferry boat at the northern end of the island.

Many people, in fact, who bought land and built houses on the island bought small houses on the mainland or at least made arrangements at the Georgetown dock to moor their boat there and park their car in its parking lot so that the people would have a means of traveling to Palatka and Crescent City to buy groceries and other necessities.

More photos around Drayton Island

Bee hives on the island

The name Edelano harkens back to a much earlier name for the island.

A large dock on the west side of the island

Another dock on the east side of the island

The future of Drayton Island

In talking with various residents of Drayton Island, we have learned much. Some residents are content to let the island develop slowly, attracting the same type of people that have lived there for generations. Other people have more ambitious plans to develop parts of the island into a marina and building many more houses, especially in the southern part.

The main drawback to such development plans revolves around the ferry. Will the developers have to establish their own ferry service, especially if there are a marina and housing development at the southern end of the island? Until the issue of the ferry is resolved, large-scale development will probably not take place.

Lake George can be seen in the distance south of Drayton Island.

BIBLIOGRAPHY

Nancy Cooley Alvers and Janice Smith Mahaffey. *Our Place in Time: A Chronology*. Palatka, FL: Palatka Printing Company, 1995.

Keith H. Ashley, "Archaeological Overview of Mt. Royal," *The Florida Anthropologis*t, vol. 58: 3 – 4 (September – December 2005), pp. 265 – 286.

John Bartram. *Diary of a journey through the Carolinas, Georgia, and Florida: from July 1, 1765, to April 10, 1766*. Philadelphia: The American Philosophical Society, 1942.

Bill Belleville. *River of Lakes: A Journey on Florida's St. Johns River*. Athens, GA: University of Georgia Press, 2000.

Edmund Berkeley and Dorothy Smith Berkeley. *The Life and Travels of John Bartram: From Lake Ontario to the River St. John*. Tallahassee, FL: University Presses of Florida, 1982.

Robin C. Brown. *Florida's First People: 12,000 Years of Human History*. Sarasota, FL: Pineapple Press, 1994.

Michael V. Gannon. *The Cross in the Sand: The Early Catholic Church in Florida, 1513 – 1870*. Gainesville: University of Florida Press, 1965.

Frank Hays, "Drayton Islanders Get Their Mail Special Delivery," *Daytona Beach Sunday News*, Sept. 11, 1983.

Bob H. Lee. *Backcountry Lawman: True Stories from a Florida Game Warden*. Gainesville: University Press of Florida, 2013.

Stefan Lorant, editor. *The New World: The First Pictures of America*. New York: Duell, Sloan & Pearce, c. 1946.

Philip S. May, "Zephaniah Kingsley, Nonconformist (1765 – 1843)," *The Florida Historical Quarterly*, vol. 23, no. 3 (January 1945), pp. 145 – 159.

Kevin M. McCarthy. *Native Americans in Florida.* Sarasota, FL: Pineapple Press, 1999.

Kevin M. McCarthy. *St. Johns River Guidebook,* 2nd edition. Sarasota, FL: Pineapple Press, 2008.

Kevin M. McCarthy. *Thirty Florida Shipwrecks.* Sarasota, FL: Pineapple Press, 1992, pp. 68 – 71, "Columbine, 1864."

John T. McGrath. *The French in Early Florida: In the Eye of the Hurricane.* Gainesville: University Press of Florida, 2000.

Brian E. Michaels. *The River Runs North: A History of Putnam County.* Dallas, TX: Taylor Publishing Company, 1976.

Jerald T. Milanich, editor. *Famous Florida Sites: Mount Royal and Crystal River.* Gainesville: University Press of Florida, 1999.

Jerald T. Milanich. *Florida's Indians from Ancient Times to the Present.* Gainesville: University Press of Florida, 1998.

Charles N. Mooney and others. *Soil Survey of Putnam County, Florida.* Washington: Government Printing Office, 1916.

Charles L. Mowat, "The Enigma of William Drayton," *The Florida Historical Quarterly*, vol. 22, No. 1 (Jul., 1943), pp. 3 – 33.

Edward A. Mueller. *St. Johns River Steamboats.* Jacksonville, FL: Edward A. Mueller, 1986.

Barbara A. Purdy. *The Art and Archaeology of Florida's Wetlands.* Boca Raton, FL: CRC Press, 1991.

Marjorie Kinnan Rawlings. *Cross Creek.* New York: Charles Scribner's Sons, 1942.

Daniel L. Schafer. *Anna Madgigine Jai Kingsley: African Princess, Florida Slave, Plantation Slaveowner.* Gainesville, FL: University Press of Florida, 2003.

Mark Van Doren, editor. *Travels of William Bartram.* New York: Dover Publications, Inc., 1928.

John E. Worth. *The Timucua Chiefdoms of Spanish Florida: vol. 1: Assimilation.* Gainesville: University Press of Florida, 1998.

Photo credits

The photos in this book were taken by the author, Kevin McCarthy, unless otherwise noted. Other sources: Florida Department of Environmental Protection: cover and p. 97.

Bill Jeter Jr. and Deanne Clark: pp. 1,13 (both),14 (both), 45,56,65,77,78,81,82, 83 (bottom),104 (top),105,112.

Florida State Archives, Florida Memory: pp. 4, 5,17,18,19,24,26,27 (both),28 (both),33,35,37,48,60,62,69,72 (both), 83 (top),86,88,93.

Karl Musser: p. 3.

SMBishop: p. 15.

TampAGS, for AGS Media: p. 20.

Averette at English Wikipediap: p. 31.

Library of Congress: p. 32.

The Florida Center for Instructional Technology, University of South Florida: p. 34.

N. Orr: p. 36.

Daniel Mayer: p. 38.

Howard Pyle: p. 39.

Internet: p. 51.

Tom Fawls: p. 54.

Bill Trotter: p. 55.

Jim Cusick: p. 67.

Wilfredo R Rodriguez H.: p. 73.

Walt Grampp: pp. 89,90,91,94, 96.106.

Bruce Geiger: p. 103.

Matisse: p. 116.

To the right: co-authors
Walt Grampp (on the left)
and Kevin McCarthy

About the authors

Walt Grampp graduated from the University of Connecticut in 1956 and served in the Medical Corps of the U.S. Army (1956 – 1958), then was in the nursery field with a partner (1958 – 1967). He founded and operated Shadow Lake Nursery (1967 – 1976). The nursery was well known for the high quality of plants and also the degree of mechanization he achieved. Groups of out-of-state nursery groups toured the operation. During that time he represented the State of New Jersey in the American Nursery Association and traveled around the country giving talks. He then started Horticultural Automation: Walt Grampp & Associates. He represented equipment manufacturers and had a line of conveyers made in a plant in Pinellas Park, Florida. He operated an under-ground lawn sprinkler company, Monmouth Sprinkler Company (1970 – 1975). Walt, a third-generation Drayton Islander, has long had an interest in the rich history of Drayton Island. He is a board member of the Bartram Trails Society and was active in the marker project. He is also a member of the St. Augustine Historical Society, the Fruitland Historical Society, and is a trustee of the Marjorie Kinnan Rawlings Society.

Kevin McCarthy earned his B.A. in American Literature from LaSalle College (1963), his M.A. in English from the University of North Carolina – Chapel Hill (1966) and his Ph.D. in Linguistics from the same school (1970). He taught in the Peace Corps in Turkey for two years, in Lebanon as a Fulbright Professor for one year, in Saudi Arabia as a Fulbright Professor for two years, and as a professor of English and Linguistics at the University of Florida for 33 years. He has had 64 books published, mostly about Florida, plus several dozen articles in scholarly and popular journals and has given over 300 talks to schools and academic groups. For more about his publications see his web site: www.kevinmccarthy.us. In 2003 the University of Florida named him its Distinguished Alumni Professor. Since retiring from the University of Florida in 2005, he has taught writing workshops in Hanoi, Vietnam two times and has taught English-as-a-Foreign Language in Spain four times. He continues to research and write nonfiction books.

Index

Made in the USA
Middletown, DE
24 January 2022

59575675R00073